DAD & ME

SETTING FARTS FREE

WRITTEN AND ILLUSTRATED BY
JANE BEXLEY

ISBN 9798745521416

My dad is the coolest and I'll prove it to you.
There's no end to the marvelous things he can do!

He can fix anything. He's kind, brave, and tough.
He sings when he cleans; all that awesome dad stuff.

On top of all that, there's one skill where he shines above all other dads, and I'm so proud he's mine.

HE FARTS. Yes, he farts! How's that special you wonder? You must not have encountered his mega bum thunder.

He can blow big, he can squeak small,
With his wide range of toots he out-gasses them all.

He uses cheek squeakers with careful precision
and turns movie nights into smell-o-vision.

When our favorite song makes us jump to our feet,
he plays the bum drum and drops with the beat.

He's super silly and tells fart jokes with ease,
never missing the chance to ask...

On road trips we don't often get very far
before silent but deadly toot clouds fill the car.

I'll be just like him one day, if I give it my best.
I'll master my fart skills before leaving the nest.
Dad says he will teach me his cheek-flapping ways,
but it will take work and some long nights and days.

We'll train for hours with our trusty dart guns,
and score double points with the pews from our buns.

We'll prep our rump rockets to blast into space
by fueling our engines with beans by the case.

We'll meet the gas giants and talk about fumes
until we run out of our trusty legumes.

Then after our flight we'll come back down to earth and we'll let some more rip while we tear up the turf.

And when we are done fumigating the grass, we'll hop on his bike and I'll yell...

... HIT THE GAS!

VRROOOOM!

I want my glute toots to be big and strong too. So I'll do extra practice when he's not in view.

I'll eat gassy foods to increase my fart size, I'll fine tune my aim, Dad will be so surprised!

I'll save up my gas when he's in the next room,
then sneakily enter to launch a huge...

"Are you okay?" Dad gently inquired.
"In more ways than one, that really backfired.
I know you can't wait to do things just like me,
But there's plenty of time to become who you'll be!"

And he's right of course, that wise dad of mine.
My booty will blow bigger fluffs with more time.
And I'll grow in more ways than just making farts loud
while I work towards the day...

...when my toots make him proud.

Made in United States
North Haven, CT
25 May 2022

19535420R00022